Not Oatmeal
Hikes The Appalachian Trail

Written by Opye Bettis
Illustrated by Youssef Rahmaoui

Copyright © 2025 Delack Media Group LLC
All rights reserved.

This book may not be reproduced in whole or any part without the expressed written consent of the publisher. No part of this publication may be reproduced, stored in a retrieval system, or transmitted in any form or by any means—electronic, mechanical, photocopying, recording, or otherwise—without the prior written permission of the publisher.

This is a work of creative nonfiction. Some names, characters, places and incidents are either the product of the author's imagination or can be used fictitiously, and any resemblance to actual persons, living or dead, business establishments or brands, events or locales is entirely coincidental.

Written by Opye Bettis
Cover design and Illustrations by Youssef Rahmaoui
Published by Delack Media Group LLC
www.delackmediagroup.com

This book is dedicated to my Mom.

She's my hero.

My name's Not Oatmeal.
I'm four years old.

Wanna hear how I walked all the way from Georgia to Maine?

It all started at Amicalola Falls in Georgia. I got my very own purple tag: number 887.

Then I climbed 604 stairs straight up a waterfall (my legs were not impressed).

At Springer Mountain, I saw the first white blaze of the Appalachian Trail. It looked just like a secret code.

But it's really a white marker on a tree. It helps you to know which way to go.

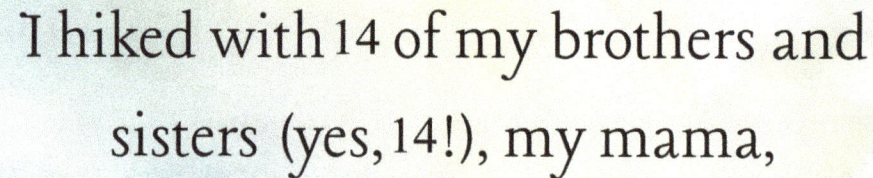

I hiked with 14 of my brothers and sisters (yes, 14!), my mama,

and our adopted dog Lulu.
Her trail name is Q-tip.

One night,
it got SOOOOOOO COLD,
the wind bit my nose!

The next morning, icicles were hanging from the rocks —
Taller than ME!
I felt like a popsicle with a backpack.

It rained aaaaaaaa LOT. But rain means salamanders.
People call them efts.
I caught hundreds of them.

I also built fairy houses with my acorn fairy family.
Acorn Mom was very bossy.

I kayaked in a lake in Tennessee, hiked up green mountains in North Carolina, and saw the wild, Grayson Highland ponies in Virginia.

I waved from bridges so all the cars and trucks honked. Helloooooo!

Hi trucks! Bye trucks!
Hi Cars! Bye cars!

At mile 848, I slipped on a wet rock.
BAM. OUCH! Head bump.

My sister fixed me up with a bandage.
I love my sister.

I climbed lots and lots of really big mountains

I walked through green fields where cows ate grass,

climbed on lots of rocks,

and slid down waterfalls like a slide
YEEEEHAAAAAAA

We saw a mama bear AND her babies that day.

But wanna know the coolest part?
A cute little frog in a tiny cave!
RIBBIT

I saw lots of snakes.

Butterflies even landed on my fingers.

Snow.

Sleet.

Rain. Hail.
BAM! OUCH!
That hail hurt!
The weather didn't always cooperate.

In Pennsylvania, we saw mushrooms in all colors of the rainbow

I climbed lots of fire towers

and rock climbed up huge mountains in New Hampshire.

The wind even knocked me over on Mt. Washington.

You wanna know something?
I got something super rare - a super special permit to climb
Mt. Katahdin, the last mountain on the trail.
They called it an "Elite Athlete" permit.
I hiked every step - all 31,000 of them - to get to the top.

I climbed all the way up, stood on the sign,
and smiled so big my cheeks hurt.
I did it!

I finally did it! I walked 2,198.4 miles on my own two feet!
People said I couldn't do it because I was too little.
But I did and I reached the end of the trail.

I was sad to leave the Appalachian trail.
I miss the hiking. But I really miss my tent.
I love storms and stories and campfires.
I met so many new friends
I love trail life.

My name is Not Oatmeal.
I'm the youngest person to officially hike the whole Appalachian Trail.
I got blisters, bug bites, hornet stings, and stitches.
But I also got stronger, braver, and happier.
And guess what?
You can do big things too.

Explore the outdoors with me!

I'd love to see photos of you exploring the world.
Post your photo online and use the hashtag #NotOatmeal